I Want to Be a TRILLIONAIRE When I Grow Up

ACTIVITY BOOK

NEENA RANI SPEER, ESQ.

I DECLARE

I WILL MAKE TRILLIONS

THIS IS MY BOOK, AND I WILL TREAT IT WITH CARE

My Name is: _____

In this book, I will dedicate myself to learning more, trying to answer the questions I don't know, and pushing myself to think outside the box. I know each lesson day I will face 4 questions that will make me a smarter and more financially savvy student, and when I get to the end I will have learned how to (1) Budget Money, (2) Save Money, and (3) Managing Money using mathematical principles and problem solving

Neena the LAST Brand, LLC

All Rights Reserved. No part of this publication may be reproduced in any form or by any means, including scanning, photocopying, or otherwise without the publisher's prior written permission.

Disclaimer and Terms of Use: The Author and Publisher have strived to be as accurate and complete as possible in the creation of this book, notwithstanding the fact that they do not warrant or represent at any time that the contents within are accurate due to the rapidly changing nature of the internet. While all attempts have been made to verify information provided in this publication, the Author and the publisher assume no responsibility for errors, omissions, or contrary interpretation of the subject matter herein. Any perceived slights of specific persons, peoples, or organizations are unintentional. In practical advice books, like anything else in life, there are no guarantees of income made. Readers are cautioned to rely on their judgment about their circumstances to act accordingly. This book is not intended for use as a legal, business, accounting, or financial advice source. All readers are advised to seek the services of competent professionals in the legal, business, accounting, and finance fields. This is for informational use only. Not legal advice. An attorney-client relationship is not formed by viewing and receiving information attached to The Neena R. Speer Law Firm LLC's social media pages @neenarspeerlawfirm. "No representation is made that the quality of the legal services to be performed is greater than the quality of legal services performed by other lawyers."

For information on quantity sales: Special discounts are available on quantity purchases for corporations, associations, U.S. trade bookstores, wholesalers, and independent booksellers.

Copyright © 2022 Neena the LAST Brand LLC

All Rights Reserved.
ISBN: 978-1-7366939
ISBN-13: 978-1-7366939-4-0

I PROMISE TO

- DEFINE MY GIFTS
- TELL THE TRUTH
- SHARE MY STORY
- HIT MY GOALS
- CREATE AN ACTION PLAN
- TEST MY SUCCESS
- LIST OUT MY RESULTS

QUIZ

Check Your NeNe Trillionaire Smarts

TRILLIONAIRE QUIZ

Please fill out the 4 questions under each lesson to the best of your ability. This workbook will be graded separately.

Values + Money Guiding Lesson Worksheet

Name: _____ Date: _____ Grade: _____

1. What do you value?

Wants	Needs	Luxury

2. How did you grow up?

Money Struggle	Money Budget	Money Everywhere

3. What do you value?

IDK (Basic)	Kinda (Middle)	I Love It (Expert)

4. Math Riddle/Problem Solving Question of the Day:

I Want to Be A Trillionaire When I Grow Up

Social Media + Money Guiding Lesson Worksheet

Name: _____ Date: _____ Grade: _____

1. What app(s) can you use to make money?

$ Apps	Apps to Chose from	Job You Chose
	TikTok | Clubhouse | IG | Facebook | LinkedIn | Snapchat | Discord | Google Meet | Zoom | Airmeet | YouTube | DaCast | Podia | Kajabi | Teachable | SamCart	

2. Where do you spend the most time on social media…

Choices	Most Time	Least Time
Dancing, Creating, Content, Scrolling, Watching, Selling, Cannot Use		

3. Math Problem of the Day…

Problem	Your Guess	Correct Answer

4. Math Riddle/Problem Solving Question of the Day:

Jobs + Money Guiding Lesson Worksheet

Name: _____   Date: _____   Grade: _____

1. What is the average salary for your "assigned" job?

Your Skills	Dream Jobs to Choose from	Job You Chose
	Lawyer | Doctor | Nurse | Chef | Astronaut | Writer | Author | Pro Athlete | Accountant | Farmer | Scientist | Hair Stylist | Barber | Veterinarian | Teacher	

2. Name 3 People you know who are in your assigned career field...

PERSON 1	PERSON 2	PERSON 3

3. Math Problem of the Day...

Problem	Your Guess	Correct Answer

4. Math Riddle/Problem Solving Question of the Day:

I Want to Be A Trillionaire When I Grow Up

Intro to Biz + Money Guiding Lesson Worksheet

Name: _____ Date: _____ Grade: _____

1. How Old Was the Kid Who Invented Popsicles?

Name	When did they invent it?	Age

2. How old do you have to be on a board or a director of a biz?

Your Guess	Your Opinion	Correct Answer

3. Math Problem of the Day...

Problem	Your Guess	Correct Answer

4. Math Riddle/Problem Solving Question of the Day:

ACTIVITY BOOK

Trademarks + Money Guiding Lesson Worksheet

Name: _____ Date: _____ Grade: _____

1. What does ® mean?

®	ITEM YOU FOUND	What is cool about it?

2. What is something that can be trademarked?

Guess 1	Guess 2	Guess 3

3. Math Problem of the Day...

Problem	Your Guess	Correct Answer

4. Math Riddle/Problem Solving Question of the Day:

I Want to Be A Trillionaire When I Grow Up

Copyrights + Money Guiding Lesson Worksheet

Name: _____   Date: _____   Grade: _____

1. What does © mean?

[   ]

2. How much money can you sue for by law if you protect your brand with a copyright?

[   ]

3. Math Problem of the Day…

Problem	Your Guess	Correct Answer

4. Math Riddle/Problem Solving Question of the Day:

[   ]

Patents + Money Guiding Lesson Worksheet

Name: _____ Date: _____ Grade: _____

1.   What shoe has a "design" patent?

2.   How long does a patent last before it releases to the public?

3.   Math Problem of the Day...

Problem	Your Guess	Correct Answer

4.   Math Riddle/Problem Solving Question of the Day:

I Want to Be A Trillionaire When I Grow Up

Education + Money Guiding Lesson Worksheet

Name: _____ Date: _____ Grade: _____

1. How Much does it Cost to go to?

Name	Dream Jobs to Choose from	Job You Chose
	• Barber School • Cosmetology School • Community College • 4-Yr Public College • 4- Yr. Private College • Acting School	

2. What is the cost of a good laptop?

3. Math Problem of the Day…

Problem	Your Guess	Correct Answer

4. Math Riddle/Problem Solving Question of the Day:

Pg. 13

ACTIVITY BOOK

Struggling + Money Guiding Lesson Worksheet

Name: _____ Date: _____ Grade: _____

1. What does it mean to go bankrupt?

What famous rapper do you know filed for bankruptcy? What about the Basketball player?

3. Math Problem of the Day...

Problem	Your Guess	Correct Answer

4. Math Riddle/Problem Solving Question of the Day:

I Want to Be A Trillionaire When I Grow Up

Debt + Money Guiding Lesson Worksheet

Name: _____ Date: _____ Grade: _____

Should you get a credit card in college, high school, grad school, or wait until you become an older adult?

[ ]

My business was affected by the pandemic, and I asked for a EIDL (Loan). Do I have to pay them back?

[ ]

3. Math Problem of the Day...

Problem	Your Guess	Correct Answer

4. Math Riddle/Problem Solving Question of the Day:

[ ]

Investing + Money Guiding Lesson Worksheet

Name: _____ Date: _____ Grade: _____

1. How much does it cost to buy 1 stock share from Starbucks?

   [   ]

2. Can you invest in a business and make money from it?

   [   ]

3. Math Problem of the Day...

Problem	Your Guess	Correct Answer

4. Math Riddle/Problem Solving Question of the Day:

   [   ]

I Want to Be A Trillionaire When I Grow Up

Planning + Money Guiding Lesson Worksheet

Name: _____ Date: _____ Grade: _____

1. What lifestyle do you aim to live?

Name	Lifestyle to Choose from	Your Choice
	• Celebrity Status ($1,000,000 +) • Comfortable and Rich ($150,000 -$999,000) • Middle Class ($60,000-$149,999) • Gets the Job Done ($20,000- $59,999) • Struggles But Can Still be Happy ($0-$19,999)	

2. Based on how you want to live, what should your 219 working days rate be?

_____ ÷ 219 = _____ ??

Your choice

3. Math Problem of the Day...

Problem	Your Guess	Correct Answer

4. Math Riddle/Problem Solving Question of the Day:

Neena Speer

Financial Literacy Consultant

Money Game

Worksheets

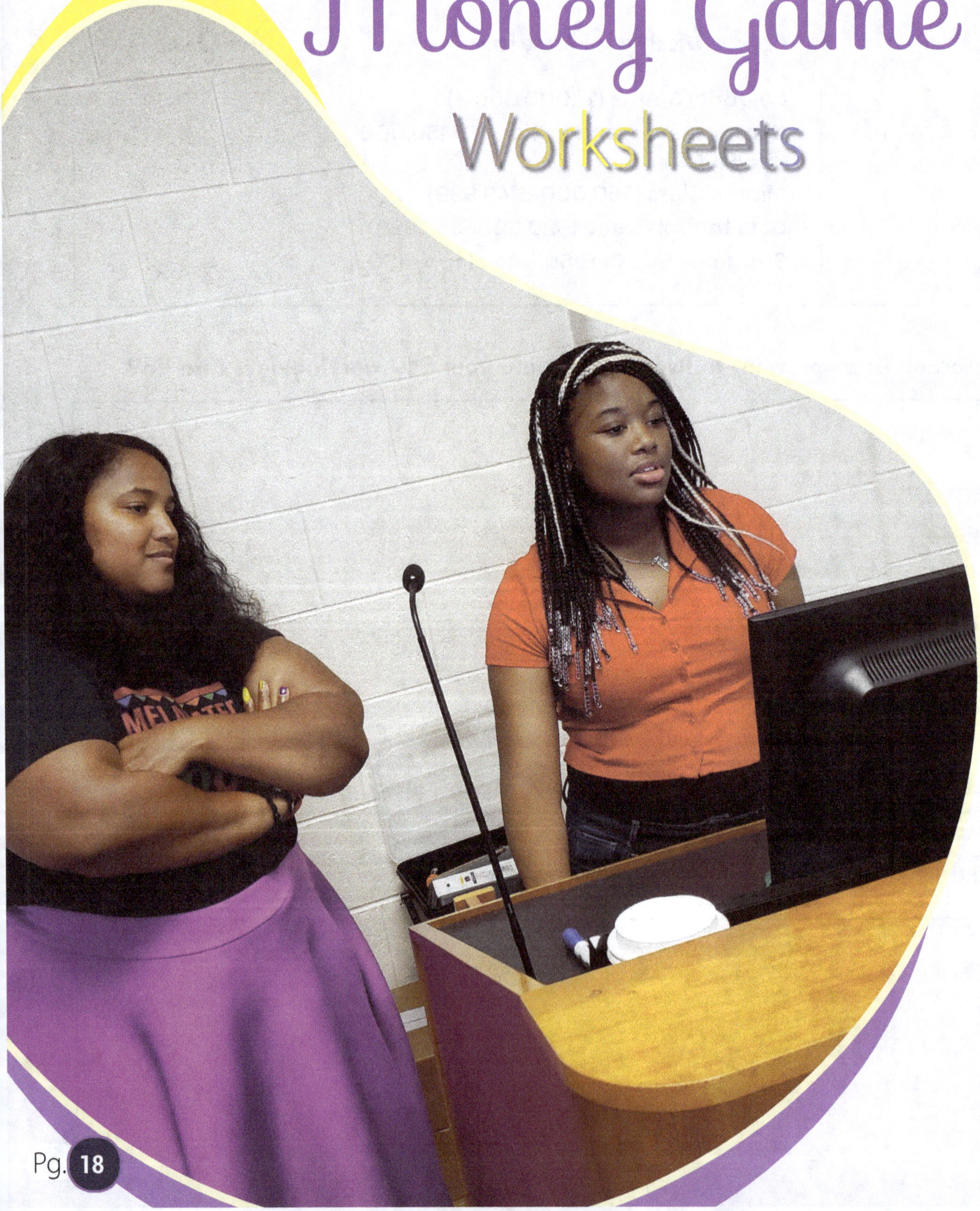

Dollar and Dream Activity

SMART GOALS

SPECIFIC
MEASURABLE
ACHIEVABLE
RELEVANT
TIME BASED

HOW MUCH MONEY DO YOU PHYSICALLY HAVE $_____

HOW CAN YOU DOUBLE IT?

TEST MY SUCCESS

NAME YOUR IDEA

LIST OUT MY RESULTS

CAN YOU COME UP WITH SOMETHING SIMPLE THAT MAKES THE MOST MONEY WITH WHAT YOU HAVE

Play Spent Game

WHAT HARD DECISIONS DID YOU MAKE?

PICK YOUR JOB TO START

DETERMINE HOW FAR YOU WILL LIVE FROM WORK

WHAT WERE EASIER DECISIONS FOR YOU TO MAKE?

PICK YOUR HEALTH CARE PLAN

YOU HAVE TO MAKE $1000 LAST UNTIL THE END OF THE MONTH

WOULD YOU CHANGE THE DECISION IF YOU HAD AN EXTRA $1000 COMING IN PER MONTH?

I Want to Be A Trillionaire When I Grow Up

The Bean Game

YOU NEED 20 UNCOOKED BEANS TO START

DRAW ABOUT 20 CIRCLES ON YOUR PAPER

YOU CANNOT GET MORE BEANS UNLESS TOLD YOU CAN BY THE "BEAN BANKER" WITH THE TEST

15-20 SCENARIO STATEMENTS WILL BE READ AFTER YOU HAVE PLACED ALL YOUR BEANS

DID YOU HAVE TO DOWNGRADE OR TAKE THINGS AWAY TO STAY ON THE BOARD?

WHERE DID YOU TAKE BEANS FROM FIRST?

WHAT IF YOU STARTED WITH 40 BEANS?

Savings Plan

ON A SHEET OF PAPER WRITE THE $ AMT EVERYTIME YOU ADD OR TAKE MONEY AWAY

GET A JAR OR BIG MOUTH BOTTLE OF ORANGE JUICE AND CLEAN IT OUT

BRING IT IN

TELL ME ABOUT YOUR FIRST BIG PURCHASE

START WITH SOMETHING WORTH $20-$99 THE FIRST TIME

LET'S PAINT IT !

HOW MUCH COULD YOU SAVE AND NOT SPEND IN A YEAR?

WRITE ON THE OUTSIDE YOUR SAVINGS ITEM

I Want to Be A Trillionaire When I Grow Up

I Want to Make.......

WHAT CAN YOU DO TO MAKE $ _____ PER DAY?

A. $ _____ / YEAR

B. $ _____ / DAY

= A/219 = _____ = B

WHAT EXPENSIVE THINGS DO YOU WANT TO BUY EVERY YEAR?

B. PER DAY $ _____
3 JOBS THAT EARN THIS PER DAY

HOW MANY HOURS A DAY WILL YOU WORK?

WHAT WILL IT COST YOU TO LIVE?

ACTIVITY BOOK

BUSINESS Canvas

COSTS/ EXPENSES

BUSINESS NAME

BUSINESS TYPE

UNFAIR ADVANTAGE

BRAND STORY

WHY YOU STARTED IT

KEY PARTNERS

Make My Own Money

Cash	Coin

My First Budget Sheet

Date	Description of Task Expense	Amount	Amount Left

I Want to Be A Trillionaire When I Grow Up

Activate My Smarts
My First Savings Chart

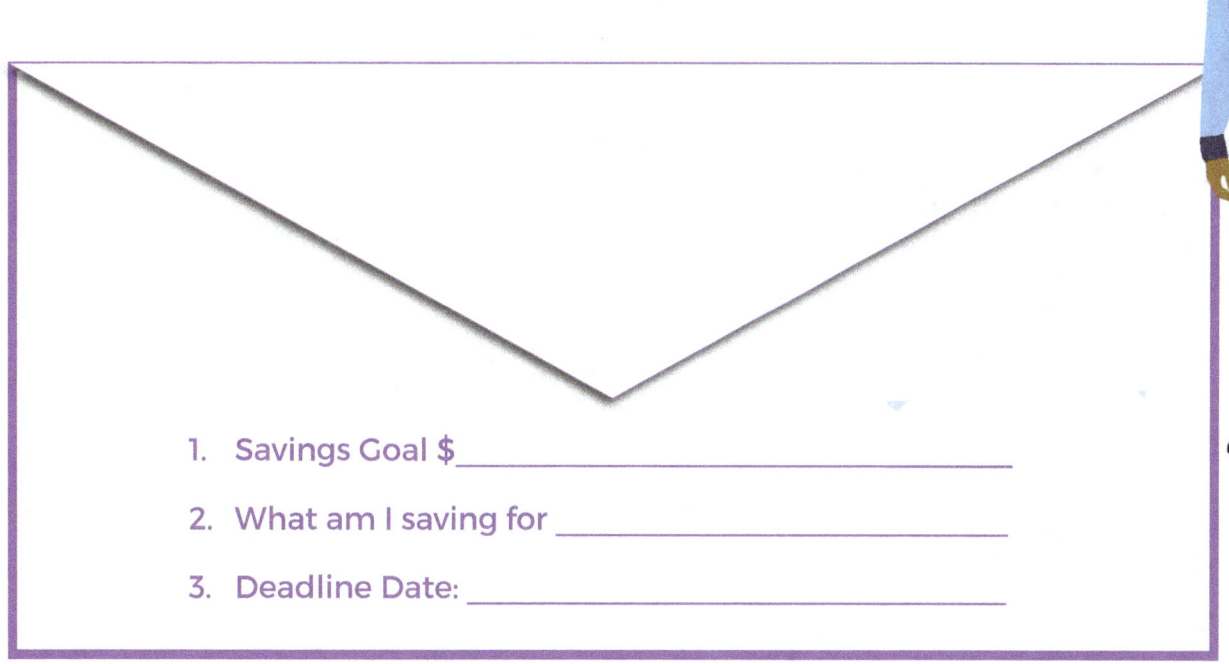

1. Savings Goal $_____
2. What am I saving for _____
3. Deadline Date: _____

Date	Amount Saved	How Much is Left to Save	How many days left

ACTIVITY BOOK

ACTIVATE My Smarts

My First Money Manager

Date	Description	Amount	Amt to Donate?	Amt to Put in Piggybank?	Amt to Buy Something?

I Want to Be A Trillionaire When I Grow Up

The Words of NeNe Trillionaire

```
J N D X F G Q M T R A D E M A R K N B F
T H S N Y K T S H B X U S Y V P M N O A
W H A V H E V X X T Y S C R N C A Y O F
P Z T G I P Y N E O V N H A R Y I S K S
R H O P A S C S C U Q A O L J L L T K A
P A T E N T R U Z E H O L A V U I O E J
T S B U D G E T I N G L A S D Q N C E G
S N R C J Q D F N H D Z M R F T J G K N
E T L E I G I L R L I C S Y H W Q S P I
R A Z N T N T S O H L H H N G R U M R T
E X R Y A I Q C Q D K C I O I L E A D S
T E G Q W V R Y L A B T P I R J L F E E
N S B S H A R E W E U I N S Y G P P B V
I Z U Z A S G X M L S P S R P R A A T I
L A Y A W A Y E H E I H Y E O A Y Y N J
C H E C K B O O K P N Z E V C N R C Q J
F I N A N C I N G H E T N N T O H R X T
E M E R G E N C Y X S P O O R S L E B W
A C C O U N T A N T S N M C L C L C E T
E V S I K E H P Q C N C F B P E Y K W O
```

1. Magnets	11. Investing	21. Layaway
2. Lists	12. Stocks	22. Financing
3. Leads	13. Checkbook	23. Credit Score
4. Conversion	14. Trademark	24. Budgeting
5. Money Market	15. Copyright	25. Saving
6. Bookkeeper	16. Patent	26. Money
7. Share	17. Scholarship	27. Business Plan
8. LLC	18. Common App	28. Pitch Deck
9. Debt	19. Interest	29. Consulting
10. Credit	20. Credit Card	30. Salary

Draw Yourself As A Trillionaire

Instructions: Becoming a Trillionaire takes time but remember the richest people are kind and caring even when it's hard. They try to budget so they don't overspend. They try to save so they have money for a hard day. They try to manage money well so they can do more positive things in this world. So imagine a kind and caring money smart Trillionaire when you're drawing

Meet The AUTHOR

ABOUT THE VISION

I equip Title 1 students with the tools to become financially savvy using mathematical principles and problem solving skills through budgeting, saving, and managing money.

Neena tells her story about how she was born to thrive, not survive, when she nearly lost her life at 6 years of age due to chickenpox encephalitis and how her life has been both amazing in a loving home but riddled with obstacles she never imagined. By the age of eight, Neena came up with her first business training manual to pitch to a local non-profit. She worked on it and tried to get it implemented before she graduated high school, but no one would listen to her BIG IDEAS. She kept on creating programming and acting as the proxy leader for many organizations throughout her career, but people would not let her lead. So, she did what any financial genius would do next, "created her own business," but that happened after she did what others wouldn't. Learn the game.

Neena did the busy work, learned the inventory process, and went behind the scenes of many organizations and figured out how to make their systems more efficient. When she went to Howard University, she launched her very own MATH TUTORING business, after many unpaid invoices and IOU's, she finally started tutoring athletes in Math and French formally with Howard Athletics, and that's when teaching math in a fun and unique way began. Her method of applying her knowledge to teaching financial literacy became something powerful.

In Freshman year, she learned that hustling ain't all it's cracked up to be if you don't understand the business behind it. After growing up with a life-long YMCA relationship as a baby in the nursery, to after school, to volunteering, to counselor in training, to nursery worker, to nine years as summer camp counselor.

She not only loves kids, but she worked at a non-profit long enough to learn everything she needed to start her own because her bosses had her create counselor schedules, camper schedules, do inventory, and yes even paint some picnic benches without a single complaint from her. Neena uses what she learned to empower kids to learn more about the amazing power of math and problem solving to understand money, business, leadership and making millions.